Boys in My Eyes

God's Thoughts on Boys and Men

By Issachar Nichols

Scripture taken from the (NASB®) NEW AMERICAN STANDARD BIBLE, Copyright © NASB 1960, 1962, 1963, 1968, 1971, 1972, 1973, 1975, 1977, 1985 by The Lockman Foundation. Used by permission. All rights reserved. lockman.org

Scripture taken from the (NASB®) NEW AMERICAN STANDARD BIBLE, Copyright © NASB 1960, 1962, 1963, 1968, 1971, 1972, 1973, 1975, 1977, 1985, 1995 by The Lockman Foundation. Used by permission. All rights reserved. lockman.org

Scripture taken from the (NASB®) NEW AMERICAN STANDARD BIBLE, Copyright © NASB 1960, 1962, 1963, 1968, 1971, 1972, 1973, 1975, 1977, 1985, 1995, 2020 by The Lockman Foundation. Used by permission. All rights reserved. lockman.org

Scriptures quotations taken from The Holy Bible, New International Version® (NIV®). Copyright © 1973, 1978, 1984, 2011, by Biblica, Inc.® Used with permission. All rights reserved worldwide.

Scripture quotations from THE MESSAGE. Copyright © by Eugene H. Peterson 1993, 2002, 2005, 2018. Used by permission of NAVPress. All rights reserved.

Scripture quotations are taken from the Holy Bible, New Living Translation, Copyright © 1996, 2004, 2007, 2013 by Tyndale House Foundation. Used by permission of Tyndale House Publishers, Carol Stream, Illinois.

King James Version (KJV) 1769 KING JAMES VERSION, public domain.

All scripture references and translations appear in the Endnotes. Quotes and references appear in the Endnotes. Used by permission. All rights reserved.

Hardcover edition:
ISBN: 979-8-9992481-4-5
Paperback edition:
ISBN: 979-8-9992481-3-8
Ebook edition:
ISBN: 979-8-9992481-2-1
Imprint: Issachar&Jesus
Cover design: Maddie Cabibbo
Photographer: David Gorodetskiy

ENDORSEMENTS

A book with a big heart. A book with practical wisdom. Issachar pours out her passion for young men to know and trust Jesus and walk in their identity with Him. With powerful truths, boys are reminded that "you are strong, and the word of God lives in you, and you have overcome the evil one" (1 John 2:14). Boys (and parents of these gifts) are prompted about questions young people ask and given tools and declarations to bring hope and power to overcome! Thanks, Issachar, for putting your compassion and wisdom on pages!

Paul and Susan Kummer
Bethel Leaders Network, Redding, CA
Authors of " Equipping the Saints: Raising Up Everyday
Revivalists Who Sustain the Move of God."
Ages: 62 and 53

I've had the privilege of growing up with Issachar in my life from an early age, and it's been inspiring to watch her grow into the bold, thoughtful, and compassionate leader she is today. Her deep love for Jesus is evident not only in her words, but in the way she lives. This book is a reflection of that devotion. Issachar writes with a heart full of faith and a voice from the Lord.

Axel Kibby
Age: 22

Author Issachar Nichols brings God's heart to the pages, for young boys as well as grown men, in her book, Boys in My Eyes!! And I can say she saves the best for the last part in this book, as it got better and better the more I read!

Mark Newman
Age: 41

A theme that is shown throughout this book is that God does not want us to wait. So many young boys and men have fallen for the lie that we are too young and not prepared, that we are waiting to reach a certain age or life milestone before we can truly live the life God has planned for us. This lie keeps young boys and men stagnant and complacent. This unfortunately has been true in my own life. But we know this is a lie because Jesus didn't live this way when he was a boy. There are so many ways we can serve the Lord as young boys and men. Honoring our parents, caring for our words, and understanding our gifts and roles as boys. These were all key takeaways that boys can start practicing right now. We don't have to wait! Issachar has provided excellent insight on a young boy's life and that has come from her years of nurturing young boys in the faith. I know this because I was one of those young boys. Today many young boys and men are subject to spiritual attacks from the enemy. This book offers guidance to the Lord's truth that our young boys and men need.

Avery Kibby
Age: 24

TABLE OF CONTENTS

DEDICATION AND DECLARATION

I dedicate this book first and foremost to Jesus. And I dedicate this book to all boys that are boys, boys that are men now and boys to come.

I declare that this book will bring many sons to glory, to their true self in God and true calling.

What Jesus died for is theirs in full - if they choose it. I bless them to choose Him. May God fulfill His truths and promises over every boy and man who reads this book. I pray God would breathe His Life and Freedom into them in Jesus name. I pray every boy and man who reads this book - would come to know, love and believe in Jesus and His great love for them.

My prayer and declaration for this book is that boys and men would know who they are in God and from that place families would be restored, healed and thriving. And that you, reader, would know the power that you carry that is from God and who He says you are.

Boys have everything they need inside them from Jesus to be the men they are called to be. Jesus is the One that calls them out, champions them, disciples them and makes them into the men He created them to be. This book goes after what Jesus goes after for boys that will be men and men that have the boy inside of them that needs to be encouraged and championed. We will discover in this book some of the ways Jesus disciples boys and men.

INTRODUCTION

Dear Reader,

Welcome! I'm so glad you chose to look at this book.

I want you to know that God made you for Him and you get to live the rest of your life knowing how well He thinks of you. He is so proud of you! He wants you to know that what He has for you is beyond what you hope and dream.

Here is the story on how this book even became a book:

On January 9, 2025 God first spoke to me about writing a book. I felt a deep honor and holy heaviness from Jesus and His words about it. By His grace, here it is!

In August 2018, I went to a book writing workshop where we made space for God to speak to us about what to write. I didn't have a title at first but when I asked God for a title, I heard and wrote down "Young Boys - Boys in My Eyes." I didn't know it then, but God knew that around 7 years later I would be writing this book! So cool!

The next question was: "Why do you want to write a book on this topic?" I wrote down: "Because God has put it in my heart for a couple years now. He has given me a deep love for boys, for boys to be seen, know their value in God, know the deep love of their Father."

This is still my heart today. I'm so excited for you to be encouraged to hear God's heart for you through this book. May this book not only impact boys who are boys right now but reach the boys that are inside grown-up men, men who are still that precious boy inside, made by God.

CHAPTER 1

WHAT AM I HERE FOR? WHAT IS MY PURPOSE?

Have you ever wondered what you were made for? Or if you're going in the right direction? Am I doing what I was made to do? And how do I know if I'm doing it? I have wondered this as well. In this book, we are going to discover what God thinks of you and get more clarity and answers to these questions.

In the Bible, God says He made the work and then He made the workman: you. In Ephesians 2:10 it says, "For we are His workmanship, created in Christ Jesus for good works, which God prepared beforehand, that we should walk in them." God created good works for you to do and He created these works *before* He created you. Then, He created you so that you would walk in those good works. He prepared the work before He prepared you. He designed the work and then He designed you to fit the work you would do for His glory. And when it says "work", I believe it's work as in purpose, as in everything you do in your life! That includes your job, what you feel called to and the good things to do in your life that bless His name.

You might be picking up trash off the road as you walk by it, you might be doing sports, doing your homework or calling a friend. All of these things add up to His design for you and build character in who you are and who you are to become. The little and the big things that you do - matter; it builds character in you and gives God glory. You find out more of who you are in this process.

The Holy Spirit will guide you with His peace. He wastes nothing. You might have thought that God can't redeem a choice you made and make something beautiful out of it. But He can. There is nothing impossible for God. God is weaving the beautiful and the broken things in your life to make a beautiful story of His goodness and love. The beautiful things bring Him glory and the broken things bring Him glory too because He uses all things for good, to those who love God, and are called according to His purpose. (Romans 8:28)

God can heal and use anything to bring His love and story in your life and into others. He uses the beautiful and broken things to draw people to Himself. Your beauty and brokenness draws people to you too, because they relate to it and have it as well. We all need Jesus. He heals, redeems and purifies the beauty He has given us. He heals the brokenness in us and makes us whole. God is not afraid of our brokenness, He came to earth to heal the brokenness and save us from our sin. Through Holy Spirit, He is teaching us what it's like to be truly whole through Him. He returns us to what we are designed for. What we are designed for is holiness and wholeness, for Him.

God put you here on earth on purpose. He put you here on purpose for His purpose. And, His purpose is for you to know Him, be loved by Him and love from His heart. You are known completely by Him. How comforting that is!

Do you want to know more about your purpose? The Holy Spirit will reveal who you are to you. In Luke 2:26a it says, "And it had been revealed to him by the Holy Spirit..." The Holy Spirit reveals things to us, for us and for others. He speaks to us and reveals things to us. It is so fun living with Holy Spirit!

ASK AND RECEIVE

I remember asking God years ago to give me more awareness of His Presence and what He is aware of. And He has really answered that prayer! Some ways He gives me more awareness are the little blessings He does in the day like bringing a hummingbird across my path because He knows I love them and it reminds me that He sees me. Or someone giving me a hug as if it was Jesus hugging me through them when I needed it. Someone texting me encouragement and it was what I needed to hear that day.

It could be someone giving you a gift at a time in your life that was hard. It could be someone giving you something you've wanted and didn't tell them that you wanted it. It could be someone who gave you a smile or said something kind to you. He sees you. He's aware of what you enjoy, what makes you happy and makes you come alive. He loves letting you know that He knows you and loves you! He speaks to you through His creation and the world you live in.

It's amazing how He sees us and knows what we need in the moment we're in. It's amazing to see more of what He sees. And He wants to give you more awareness too!

He also gives us more awareness of how to love others and see them rightly in His eyes. How to bless them and let them know God loves them. He shares with us things that we can do in the moment like giving someone a smile, encouraging them, giving them a hug, sending them a text of encouragement or what you love about them etc. We get the honor of sharing with others that God sees them like He sees us. That He's aware of them and wants to let them know that He sees them.

Holy Spirit will teach and show you how to see like He does. He is our Faithful Friend and reminds us of the truth. In John 14:16-17 Jesus says, "I will ask the Father, and He will give you another Helper, that He may be with you forever; that is the Spirit of truth, who the world cannot receive, because it does not see Him or know Him, but you know Him because He abides with you, and will be in you."

Seeing like God meant us to see is what Adam and Eve traded in the Garden of Eden for seeing the way the enemy wants us to see. What Jesus did for us - when He gave His life for us and rose again gave us the ability to see again like God sees. He shows us how God sees life and everything. Praise Jesus! Every day of our lives we get to grow in this awareness of God and what He is aware of, what He sees and what matters to Him.

GOD IS WHO AND WHAT YOU ARE LOOKING FOR. HIS REST IS GROWTH.

God will catch your attention. He knows how to find you and draw you to Himself. Being the Lord's is enough. When you are the Lord's, you live out your true self in the Holy Spirit. If God is your focus, He will develop you and grow you as you grow up, if you let Him. Resting in God is the most mature thing to do. His rest is growth. You rest by believing what He says about you. Resting in His words. Believing in His words. Resting in Him.

You are made on purpose! For His glory and for your good.

YOUR MISSION TODAY

Ask Jesus to make you more aware of what He wants to reveal to you. To give you the eyes to see what He sees. Then, trust in God and choose to look for Him in your day. See what He does!

In the next chapter, we will discover more on how God guides us into our purpose.

CHAPTER 2

GOD WILL INSTRUCT YOU IN THE WAY TO GO

God says in Psalm 32:8, "I will instruct you and teach you in the way you should go; I will counsel you and watch over you."

God will show us the way to go! As we grow, He will show us what we need at the moment we need it. When we seek Him in His Word, God highlights things to us as we read. When I say highlight, I mean something sticks out in His Word the day you read it and you get to know God better as you pursue God and His Word. His Word is alive and active.

In Hebrews 4:12 it says, "For the word of God is alive and active. Sharper than any double edged sword, it penetrates even to dividing soul and spirit, joints and marrow; it judges the thoughts and attitudes of the heart."

God's Word is alive because the One Who is alive forever spoke those words into existence. Through God's disciples, those that followed Him, He spoke to them His words and they wrote them down. It is called the Bible - the Word of God.

In John chapter 1, it talks about Jesus being the Word of God. He is the Word made flesh, made human. He showed us what God is like by becoming a man Himself.

Jesus is also the Son of God. He was a boy, just like you. He relied on His Father. We have much to learn from Him. This is exciting and good news!

JESUS' WAY = HONOR

In Luke 2:51-52, it talks about Jesus and what He did as a boy and how He honored His Heavenly Father and earthly parents. It says,

"And He went down with them [his earthly parents] and came to Nazareth; and He continued in subjection to them; and His mother treasured all these things in her heart. And Jesus kept increasing in wisdom and stature, and in favor with God and men."

This is a beautiful glimpse into the boy life of Jesus. He never sinned and the things we see in His Word show us what He is like and how we can live by the power of the Holy Spirit like Jesus did. He continued in subjection, humility and honor to His earthly parents and when He did that, He honored His Heavenly Father at the same time.

Honor is powerful. Honor means respect. When you honor others, you're also honoring yourself. Because when you honor others, you're getting to experience the fullness of life God designed you to experience. I believe when you choose to honor, honor leads you to God's path for your life. God's path is honor. Honor is your portion.

The way God designed life to be is when you bless, you get blessed in return. When you honor, you get honored in return. When you bless and honor, you are blessing and honoring God and yourself. It might look different than what you think being blessed and being honored looks like, but it's the way God designed you to be as a full and whole person. As you give, you are receiving. This is part of the heart of the kingdom of God.

It also says that Jesus kept increasing in wisdom and stature. Even though He is perfect, He still increased in wisdom. This is very interesting and beautiful. It makes me think that growing in wisdom doesn't mean Jesus wasn't perfect, it's something that He and us humans grow in as we grow up. Like when you were younger, there are things now that you know that you didn't know then that have made you wiser. Growing in wisdom is part of growing as a human. And in Jesus' experience, He grew in wisdom because He was a human Himself and yet He was without sin at the same time.

Next, it says Jesus grew in favor with God and men. I understand Jesus growing in favor with men, but when I read Him increasing in favor with God, I find this interesting. I don't fully understand what this means, but I know that Jesus growing in wisdom and in favor with God, honored God and was part of Jesus' growing up.

YOU ARE A FULL PERSON

You are a full person. Even if you are a boy right now, you are still a full person. Jesus was a boy and He was fully Himself. And when Jesus was a man, He was fully Himself. He didn't become more Himself when He got older. And this is the same for you. You are fully yourself now and as you grow, you get to see more facets of yourself when you live in the full freedom God designed for you to live in. We will discover more about Jesus and His life as a boy and man in the next chapters.

My pastor Bill Johnson talks about this idea of an acorn and an oak tree. You might be like an acorn right now, but you have everything you need in you with Jesus to be that oak tree when you grow up.

AM I ON THE RIGHT PATH?

Months ago, I told two boys that I was writing a book about Boys in God's Eyes. I asked them, "What is something you would want to hear from God about?" One said, "Am I on the right path? And if I'm not, would You lead me in the right direction?" The other totally agreed that this is something he thinks about too.

This was really cool for me to hear what some boys becoming young men think about and want to hear from God about. They want to know if they're on the right path, the path that God wants them to be on. I thought that it was beautiful that those were the questions they had for God.

What I have found in my life when I have asked that question too is God has shown me that He is so pleased with me because I love Him. I actually don't want to choose something that's not of Him anymore because I have His Nature in me. I'm a new creation because of what Jesus did for me.

JESUS SET ME FREE

I remember feeling the heaviness of "Is this the right way or should I choose this or that?" "Is one better than the other?" "Is one way more pleasing to God than the other?" "What if I don't choose His best for me and don't please Him anymore?" "What if I go in a direction He doesn't want for me and I don't know it?" I remember these racing thoughts and hoping I would not have to live with that every day of my life. It felt like every day those questions were coming and I would have to answer them one way or another with my choices and decisions.

And then, Jesus took that weight off of me years ago and showed me that I don't have to live that way anymore. God revealed to me through a devotional by Oswald Chambers called *My Utmost for His Highest* (March 20, Friendship with God) that He is pleased with me and He will check me if there's something that I'm doing that He doesn't want for me or if He has something else for me.

I used to think that Him checking me was saying I'm doing something wrong but that's not what it was for. His checking me was to guide me to His best and what He had for me. He also showed me that I can choose and He is pleased either way. As long as I love Him more than anything, He is pleased. *Loving Him more than anything is what I was made for.* What a relief! The pressure is off.

The pressure is off for you too! You are made to love Him more than anything. If you love God more than anything, He will guide you because you have a relationship with Him. You love Him and He loves you. He's the Good Father, He wants to guide His children to His best for them. Sometimes, His best is you getting to choose!

There are also times when He guides me and it's more specific than other times. But most of the time, I get to choose with Him. Life has been free and sweet since He showed that to me.

And this is for you too! You may have had the same questions in your head and weren't sure what the answers were either. You also don't have to live in fear that you're going to choose something wrong every single day of your life. But you actually get to live in the true freedom that He died for for you. You can choose and He is pleased when you love Him with everything you are. He guides you with His peace.

The way He speaks to you, you'll know if it's something that needs to be paused and to hear His voice about. He will guide you, just like an earthly father guides his baby that's learning to walk. God is the Good Father. He has a unique relationship with each one of us. And He is so good at getting our attention. He will show you. His yoke is easy, and His burden is light. (Matthew 11:30)

In this chapter, we talked about honor and how it is powerful. We also talked about how God brings us to things that we get to choose with Him or He guides us into.

YOUR MISSION TODAY

What is something or someone today you are going to take time to honor? How are you gonna do that? Everything you do is worship and a present to Jesus. After you do what you are planning to do, take a second to see how it made you feel.

In the next chapter, we will be digging deeper into words and why they matter.

CHAPTER 3

YOUR WORDS MATTER AND HAVE POWER

Did you know that your words matter? That they have power? Did you know that it's not just the words you say that matter, it's also HOW you say them that matters.

What you say has power. When you speak, you can release God's atmosphere, kingdom and heart. God has also given you the power to choose Him and His kingdom or the enemy and yourself. You can either bring life or death with your tongue.

Proverbs 18:21 says this, "Death and life are in the power of the tongue: and they that love it shall eat the fruit thereof."

Another translation says this, "Words kill, words give life; they're either poison or fruit – you choose."

It is powerful that we can bring a certain kingdom just with our words. God created the world and everything we know and don't know into existence through His WORDS. If He can do that, then so can we, because we are made in His image.

Think about what God created. Animals, earth, planets, galaxies, food, water, trees and more. He created all of these with His WORDS. (Genesis chapters 1 and 2)

YOU ARE VERY GOOD

Do you know how God created human beings? Did He create them with His words? Or something else?

He created Adam and Eve with His breath and hands. (Genesis 2:7-8, Genesis 1:26-31) Isn't that amazing?! God created them not with His words, but with His breath and hands. He chose to make them in a way that was closer than His words. Distinct from everything else He made. We are His special creation, His creation that stands out above the rest. Made in God's image. Made in His likeness. Made with the breath of God. Made by the hands of God. When God created everything before man and woman, He called it good. But when He created man and woman, He called it VERY GOOD. God calls mankind VERY GOOD. I love the day when God created man and woman because He specifically says VERY GOOD. We are made in His image, we get to bless Him and reflect Him! What an honor! You are VERY GOOD in God's Eyes!!!

Psalms 139 talks about how God knows us and made us. This Psalm is like a birthday card from God to us. In verses 14 through 16 it says, "I will give thanks to You, for I am fearfully and wonderfully made; wonderful are Your works, and my soul knows it very well. My frame was not hidden from You, when I was made in secret, and skillfully wrought in the depths of the earth; Your eyes have seen my unformed substance; and in Your book were all written, the days that were ordained for me, when as yet there was not one of them."

God made you in your mother's womb! You are fearfully and wonderfully made! He is the One who weaved you together. He made you exactly the way you are for His glory and purpose. With the hair color you have, the skin color you have, the hair texture you have, your personality, your voice, your laugh, your smile…you were carefully thought out and created to bless Him and to be blessed by His Presence. You are one of a kind. There is no human that is exactly like you. God makes every human different from the other. He NEVER makes mistakes. God doesn't make duplicates. You were created on purpose. On time. Right now. For Him. To know Him. Be loved by Him. And love Him back.

BELIEVE OR NOT?

In Luke 1:20, it talks about Zacharias not believing the angel Gabriel's word about him and his wife Elizabeth having a son. So the angel said that Zacharias would be silent and unable to speak until

John, their son, was born BECAUSE he didn't believe the WORDS Gabriel said to him.

To me, this passage shows me that our words are powerful. God is bigger than our words, but He also didn't want Zacharias to say things that were not in God's heart. This shows me that what we say matters and God hears what we say and the meaning behind what we're saying. Our words can affect people either in a lifegiving way or in a way that causes death, separation, fear, sadness and bitterness. Words can either bless or hurt, bring death or life.

God was being gracious to make Zacharias silent so that he wouldn't speak unbelief anymore. And then, after John their baby was born, in Luke 1:63-79 it talks about Zacharias writing on a tablet that the baby's name is John and then his mouth was opened and his tongue made loose.

Do you know what the first thing out of his mouth was? Praise to God. He was filled with the Holy Spirit and prophesied about his son John, Jesus and

Israel. What redemption it was that Zacharias, in the Holy Spirit, spoke God's heart with his words.

Also close to this time, Mary, a relative to Zacharias and Elizabeth who was not married yet, received a word from Gabriel the same angel. He told her that she would bear a Son and name Him Jesus. In this chapter she says in Luke 1:38, "...may it be done to me according to your word..." She chose to believe and trust in God, even if it was something she didn't fully understand.

WHAT WILL YOU DO?

Be encouraged, your words matter and have power! You are made in the image of God to use your voice to bring His kingdom to earth. God has made you more powerful than you realize for His glory. What you choose to say and how you say it is meant to show what He is like. And not just to show what He is like to others, but to show what He is like to you. Your own life is a testimony of what God is like.

When you experience what He's like, you will never be the same. You will be who you are made to be fully when you allow God to live His life in you and through you.

Did you know that everything you do can give God worship? I remember a message at my childhood church where the speaker shared a story of him picking weeds outside. God was telling him that when he picks out weeds, it's an act of worship, just as much as worshiping Him during singing at church. When he said this that day, it hit me and made sense to me. It finally clicked that everything I do can bring God glory.

1 Corinthians 10:31 says this, "Whether, then, you eat or drink or whatever you do, do all to the glory of God." There's no small or big thing that outweighs the other. Everything I do, say and think can be an act of worship to Jesus. It can be something nobody sees and something everybody sees. That helped me have purpose and peace in life knowing that I can give God praise and glory through my life, whether people see what I do or not. Giving God

worship in everything and anything is like giving Him a present every time!

The point of life is knowing, loving God and giving Him worship and I can do that in EVERYTHING! And so can you! You are made to worship God in everything. When you do dishes, when you do chores, when you do your homework, when you give someone a hug, when you smile, when you acknowledge someone you pass by, when you listen, when you're present in the moment you're in, when you forgive someone…all of that and more is loving Jesus.

Matthew 25:37-40 is such a powerful part in the Bible. It describes how everything we do can be for Jesus. Part of the passage says this, "Then the righteous will answer Him [Jesus], 'Lord, when did we see You hungry, and feed You, or thirsty, and give You something to drink? And when did we see You a stranger, and invite You in, or naked, and cloth You?' The King will answer and say to them, 'Truly I say to you, to the extent that you did it to one of these brothers of Mine, even the least of them, you did it to Me.'"

We can love someone as if we're loving Jesus. What an honor. Nothing is too small that can't give Jesus worship. In this passage, it also talks about those that didn't do these things to people and therefore didn't do it unto Jesus. It's such a good reminder that Life has meaning because Jesus is The Meaning of Life.

What you do, say and think matters because it is meant to give worship to Jesus. You are meant to worship Jesus with everything you are, everything you do, everything you say and everything you think. Through Holy Spirit, this is possible. Luke 1:37 says, "For nothing will be impossible with God." Matthew 19:26 says this, "And looking at them Jesus said to them, "With people this is impossible, but with God ALL things are possible."

YOUR MISSION TODAY

Who is someone you could encourage with life-giving words today? After you encourage the person, take a moment to remember how it made you feel.

In the next chapter, we will discover more about Jesus as a boy and man and how it relates to you.

CHAPTER 4

BOY AND MAN

Jesus shows us how to be a boy and how to be a man. In the Bible, the Gospels – Matthew, Mark, Luke and John books, we discover how Jesus relied on His Father and followed Him. Jesus was born as a baby and yet was God at the same time. In Philippians 2:1-13, it talks about Jesus and how He is God and came as a Man. How He humbled Himself and became part of humanity by becoming a man. It also talks about what it is to look like Jesus. It says,

"Therefore if there is any encouragement in Christ, if there is any consolation of love, if there is any fellowship of the Spirit, if any affection and compassion, make my joy complete by being of the same mind, maintaining the same love, united in spirit, intent on one purpose. Do nothing from selfishness or empty conceit, but with humility of mind let each of you regard one another as more important than yourselves; do not merely look out for your own personal interests, but also for the interests of others. Have this attitude in yourselves which was also in Christ Jesus, who, although He existed in the form of God, did not regard equality with God a thing to be grasped, but emptied Himself, taking the form of a bond-servant, and being made in the likeness of men. Being found in appearance as a man, He humbled Himself by becoming obedient to the point of death, even death on a cross. For this reason also, God highly exalted Him, and bestowed on Him the name which is above every name, that at the name of Jesus every knee will bow, of those who are in heaven and on earth and under the earth, and that every tongue will confess that Jesus Christ is Lord, to the glory of God the Father. So then, my beloved, just as you have always obeyed, not as in my presence only, but now much more in my absence, work out your salvation with fear and trembling; for it is God who is at work in you, both to will and to work for His good pleasure."

WOW! This is a fantastic description of Jesus and what it's like when we live in Holy Spirit. To have this attitude in ourselves which was in Jesus Himself. Being humble in mind and regarding others as more important than ourselves. To do nothing out of selfishness or conceit. To think of others before ourselves.

We are made for Jesus. To give Him all the glory, to be like Him, to receive His love for us and to give His love away to all. What a mission! This is what it means to be a boy and a man after God's own heart. Just like Jesus. We are spirit beings with an earthly body. Jesus has shown us how to live as a spirit being while living in a human body Himself. He showed us the way because He is the Way. He doesn't have us figure out life on our own, He did life for us and is now doing life with us while being in us. These verses below are incredible about Jesus as well. It says,

"And He is the image of the invisible God, the first-born of all creation. For by Him all things were created, both in the heavens and on earth, visible and invisible, whether thrones or dominions or rulers or authorities - all things have been created by Him and for Him. And He is before all things, and in Him all things hold together. He is also head of the body, the church; and He is the beginning, the firstborn from the dead; so that He Himself might come to have first place in everything. For it was the Father's good pleasure for all the fullness to dwell in Him, and through Him to reconcile all things to Himself, having made peace through the blood of His cross, through Him, I say, whether things on earth or things in heaven." Colossians 1:15-20.

Jesus is the image of the invisible God! He's God made flesh, to show us how much God loves us and that through Him, and through Him alone (John 14:6), we can be made right with God again. Living in complete Unity again, one with our Creator. Forgiven and set free into who we were always meant to be in Jesus.

Because of who Jesus is and what He's done for us, we can be our full, true selves! It is only through Him that this is possible because He is God. He made us and through Jesus being God and becoming a Man for us, He gets us and knows what it's like to be a human without sin, the way we were made to be.

In the beginning, God created Adam and Eve, the first human beings without sin. Then they sinned, and we all are born into sin now and because of sin, we're separated from God and what He designed us to be in Him. And now through Jesus, we are able to be sin free, forgiven and made new. Through Jesus, we are back to who He designed us to be; no sin, Beloved Children of God, like Him, One with Him and for His glory alone.

CAN IT GET ANY BETTER?! NOPE!

Colossians 2:9-10 says, "For in Him [Jesus] all the FULLNESS of Deity dwells in bodily form, and in Him you have been made complete, and He is the head over all rule and authority;"

John 1:16 says, "For of His FULLNESS we have all received, and grace upon grace."

Ephesians 4:13 says, "Until we all attain to the unity of the faith, and of the knowledge of the Son of God, to a mature man, to the measure of the stature which belongs to the FULLNESS of Christ."

We have the fullness of God dwelling within us when we believe in Jesus. Because Jesus is the fullness of God. Wow! This is something to dwell on for the rest of our lives. We are made complete through Jesus.

ALL THE FULLNESS. OF HIS FULLNESS. TO THE FULLNESS. Wow. Wow. Wow.

Holy, Holy, Holy is the LORD God, the Almighty, who was and who is and is to come. (Revelation 4:8)

The whole earth is full of His glory. (Isaiah 6:3)

We are filled with His Glory.

JESUS AS A HUMAN

In Luke 2:40, it talks about Jesus. It says, "The Child continued to grow and become strong, increasing in wisdom; and the grace of God was upon Him."

1 Timothy 4:12 says, "Let no one look down on your youthfulness, but rather in speech, conduct, love, faith and purity, show yourself an example of those who believe."

Jesus was a baby that needed His diaper changed, needed to be taken care of, to eat food, drink water, needed hugs and comfort, love from his parents, family and friends. He grew in stature and favor with God and man. He learned how to say things. He learned how to take care of Himself as a boy and man and how to honor others. He was fully God and fully Man. He got hurt, He scraped His knee, He fell, He tripped, He cried. He learned things, learned to walk, learned to talk. He played and He laughed. He worked, He served, He said please and thank you. He got angry, He got sad, He was happy. He was misunderstood. He was seen. He slept. He needed to shower, use the bathroom and get clean physically. He needed to wash his hair, He did chores, He shared His thoughts, He had friendships.

Jesus truly gets us. He understands us. Jesus was baptized and Holy Spirit came upon Him and gave Him the strength and ability to do life victoriously as a man dependent on the Holy Spirit.

He showed us how to love people and what was important to the Father. His mission is our mission. Not to die on the cross for our sins, that was His mission for us. But we are made to be like Jesus and depend on God. Living in Holy Spirit as a new creation through the blood of Jesus. To do what Jesus did. Say what He said, think what He thinks.

And the beautiful thing is God is alive and well and still speaks. He speaks to us personally and shares with us things that He wants us to know. He also shares with us things to share with others about His heart for them. Jesus showed us that we could live as people depending and living in the strength and ability of Holy Spirit, where we can live life victoriously through Him.

DRAWN TO HIS NAME

A kindergartener boy at work was telling me, "Do you know the first time that I liked you? It was when I heard your name."

That's like God and us. We are drawn to His name, Jesus. When we hear His name, we are drawn to it because He made us.

YOUR MISSION TODAY

We have learned that Jesus understands what it's like to be a human and carry Holy Spirit at the same time. What is one way about Jesus understanding you that brings you comfort? Picture in your mind Jesus feeling comforted with you. How does that make you feel?

In the next chapter, we will discover more on how Jesus lived life victoriously and that we can too.

CHAPTER 5

IDENTITY AND POWER AS A MAN

In Luke 3:21-23 it says, "Now when all the people were baptized, Jesus also was baptized, and while He was praying, heaven was opened, and the Holy Spirit descended upon Him in bodily form like a dove, and a voice came out of heaven, "You are My beloved Son, in You I am well-pleased." When He began His ministry, Jesus Himself was about thirty years of age…"

Heaven came to earth in Jesus and Holy Spirit coming upon Him. The Father declares identity over Jesus, who Jesus is. The Holy Spirit gives Jesus power to live as a Man victoriously while being God's Son in human flesh.

God is showing us that we as human beings can be filled with the power of Holy Spirit. We can be one with God and because of that, we can live life victoriously. Without Holy Spirit we can't do life victoriously. It would be like having breath that makes you live physically, but not truly living, not fully alive.

The Father declares His identity for you. You are His son and He is well pleased with you! That is the identity you live from, from what God thinks of you.

I also find it interesting that it says Jesus began His ministry when He was about 30 years of age. When I read that, it makes me wonder if you will know by the time you're 30 what your ministry is and what you are made to do with Jesus, (it could be before or after of course). It's very possible you will be established and ready to serve in a way that's for the rest of your life. God has a special story for you to live out with Him. He has a story for you that's already planned and ready for you. Jesus will reveal it to you and be with you in the journey of life.

JESUS KNOWS THINGS

In John 2:23-25 it says, "Now when He (Jesus) was in Jerusalem at the Passover, during the feast, many believed in His name, observing His signs which He was doing. But Jesus, on His part, was not entrusting Himself to them, for He knew all men, and because He did not need anyone to bear witness concerning man, for He Himself knew what was in man."

I love how this is in the Bible. Jesus didn't trust Himself to man because He knew what was in them; the ability to sin, deceive, to not choose God, to want worship for yourself, etc. I find this powerful and cool for you to know how to live like Jesus where you love people but you trust and love God first and fully. You're aware that people can and do go astray from God. But God will never deceive you or turn away from you. He will give you discernment on how to love people. This is one reason why we need Holy Spirit. To help us know how to not put our hope in men but in God.

God is the only Being that you can truly trust. And He teaches us how to build trust between people in the right way where God is the One we ultimately trust. We can build trust with people that looks like the relationship between God and us. Jesus knew what was in man because He made them. He knows the spirit is willing, but the flesh is weak (Matthew 26:41). He is our Helper in time of need.

PROTECTOR AND PROVIDER

You are a protector and a provider. You reflect your Father in this way. In Genesis chapters 1 and 2, it talks about Adam working the garden and what he was made to do. Work is good for you. It gives you purpose, ability to grow and have something to do. And it doesn't just benefit yourself. It benefits everyone else. You are made to protect and this is so important. You protect what God made. People, animals, trees, His creation. It reflects the Father and how He protects you.

The way God designed you too with shoulders that are broad remind me of strength, protection and covering. That's some of the things you carry and how God made you that reflect Him as well.

When you don't live in your identity God made you for; to protect, provide and all the other things we've been talking about, you can tell there is something off. You are made to bless people, to show them what a boy and a man is like made in the image of God. You have a very impactful role in this life to look like Jesus and to show us what He's like as a boy and a man after God's own heart.

Boys and men that don't live in their identity can look like they don't have a purpose. They're fighting to be known, heard and loved. They don't know who they are because they don't know their Creator. They're fighting for a place to belong, looking for something that makes them feel valued and worthwhile.

You are enough. You are worthwhile. *God made you and that proves that you are worthwhile, known and loved. Jesus dying on the cross for you proves that you are worthwhile, known and loved as well.*

Jesus also showed that He is your Provider and your Protector and what that looks like. Taking care of His creation, providing grace, forgiveness, mercy, love, leadership, discipleship and so much more. He protects you from what's not His best and is the Way back to the Father. He brings us home to Him again. He took all the sin and evil of the world upon Himself on the cross so that you could be free and forgiven in Him.

God chose you. God sees you. God made you. God knows you. You have a purpose in Him. He has a beautiful story inside of you that He continues to unfold in your daily life.

GENTLENESS IS A POWER

"Your gentleness makes me great." - Psalm 18:35c. God's gentleness makes us great. There's something about gentleness that is so powerful and is one of our greatest weapons in the kingdom of heaven. It's one of the fruits of the Holy Spirit.

(Galatians 5:22-23) Romans 2:4 says, "Or do you think lightly of the riches of His kindness and forbearance and patience, not knowing that the kindness of God leads you to repentance?"

Kindness and gentleness feel super similar and yet they're both powerful and different gifts from the Lord. Kindness to me is other mindedness with love. It's doing something for others in a loving way. Gentleness to me is attached to how you do things and how you carry yourself. Gentleness is like a fragrance that people can smell and see on your life.

Gentleness has a grace. It's like a crown on a king. It graces him and shows what he carries. Like the crown, gentleness also carries authority. In my opinion, gentleness is authority with grace.

When you believe in Jesus, you carry the Holy Spirit and His fruits. Gentleness and kindness are two of the fruits of the Holy Spirit. When people see the fruits of the Holy Spirit, it's declaring who God is. You get to be a vessel where God can live in you and live through you so that people see that God loves them and is real. And He's not just real, He's for you!

You carry the gentleness and kindness of God. When you live in His Spirit, you show people what He is like. People are starving and so hungry for God, to know what He's like and to know that He loves them. They are so hungry to know why they're here, what's important, what's their purpose, what life is all about, what they are made to worship. You carry the Answer - Jesus. And through your life, they will see God.

Jesus calls Himself gentle. Matthew 11:28-30 Jesus says, "Come to Me, all who are weary and heavy-laden, and I will give you rest. Take My yoke upon you, and learn from Me, for I am *gentle* and humble in heart; and you shall find rest for your souls. For My yoke is easy, and My load is light."

If you want to be like Jesus, He is gentle and humble in heart. We are called to be like Him through Holy Spirit. Jesus in His gentleness, takes care of us, comforts us and gives us rest. He gives us His light load which is a load that is easy for us to carry. His load is our portion and is not a burden. His load is light. His light load is good for us and not heavy.

I have noticed in my life that when people are gentle with me, it leaves me space to feel safe and fully myself. It's inviting and covering. When people are gentle, it makes me want to take down my guard. It's telling me that they will treat me with gentleness, kindness, patience and respect.

When people are not gentle, it makes me want to run away from them and leaves me feeling uncovered, unsafe, scared and disrespected.

Gentleness is a big deal and we learn it from Jesus. Jesus being gentle gives us the ability to come close to Him and receive His rest and light load. His gentleness draws us to come to Him and to learn from Him.

YOUR MISSION TODAY

What is one way you can receive the gentleness of Jesus for yourself? What is one way you can be gentle to yourself today?

It could be buying yourself a treat, telling yourself in the mirror what you love about yourself, wearing your favorite clothes, playing a game you enjoy, reading a book you love, playing your favorite song. Take some time for yourself today to be gentle and bless yourself.

As you do this, remember and receive by faith the gentleness of Jesus toward you. He is gentle and loving towards you! In the next chapter, we will dig deeper into purity and see how lies don't have power over us.

CHAPTER 6

JESUS HAS MADE YOU SO PURE!

Jesus has made you so pure! It is part of your nature when you believe in Jesus. I know sometimes it doesn't feel like you are, but it's true. YOU ARE PURE! Matthew 5:8 says, "Blessed are the pure in heart, for they shall see God." Purity and seeing God are your portion! With Jesus, this is possible.

STUPID LIES!

Did you know that lies have no power over you? The only time they have power is when you GIVE power to them, when you believe they are true. Jesus has made you Pure. And if that's what He calls you, then that's what you are, because He's your Creator.

The enemy has really tried to derail me from knowing who I fully am in the Lord by attacking my purity in Jesus. Things the enemy says are: "Are you pure?" "Remember that bad thought?" "Remember that feeling?" "If people know, they'll never accept you." "If people hear about this, they'll never want to be your friend or be close to you anymore." All of these thoughts are LIES.

Over the years, I've struggled with believing that I'm pure. By the grace of God, it's getting better and better. This is one of the things God says about me, that for some reason, is hard for me to truly believe. Even though I know in my heart it's true that I am pure, my head doesn't always believe it.

The thing is, the thoughts that would come up that would make me feel not pure were actually *not my thoughts*. The enemy was throwing these thoughts up in my mind like commercials, making me think they were my thoughts when they were actually from him. The enemy was going after something that I carry which is purity and making me think that I'm not pure so that I wouldn't live in my full identity.

In the moment, it feels so real and feels like they are my thoughts. If I see it, feel it or it comes across my mind, I feel like I have no choice but to choose it, to give in to it. It makes me feel like I'm a slave to a thought and there's no way out. But it's all a LIE.

Lies make you feel like you're all alone and that there's no way out. They make you feel like you're a slave and that you're not bigger than them. *Lies make you forget God, Who is the most powerful Being.*

YOU MAKE THE ENEMY SCARED!

The enemy is actually afraid of who you are in Jesus and Him living inside of you. The enemy is trying his hardest to derail you and get your focus off of God. He knows he lost when Jesus died and rose again and he's trying his hardest to get your focus off of God so that you live a life that's less than what you were meant to live in Jesus. He doesn't want God to be glorified. He doesn't want you to know who you are in Jesus and what Jesus has ALREADY done for you. He wants you to live a life that is hidden, covered, in bondage and not fully alive. Less than God's best for you.

In John 10:10 Jesus says, "The thief (the enemy) comes only to steal, and kill, and destroy; I came that they might have life, and might have it abundantly." The enemy is all about wanting to be God and when he couldn't, he went against God. The enemy used to be Lucifer, an angel of God that worshiped God. But then, he got tempted to want to be God. He wanted to be worshiped as God. So God sent him away and now the enemy, satan, wants to hurt God. And the way he can hurt God is by hurting the image bearers of God, US. He wants us to have our focus on anything but God, even if it's a good thing. The enemy wants us to worship anything else but God. He doesn't want God to be glorified. He doesn't want God to get His full reward which is His image bearers knowing, enjoying, following, worshiping and believing in their Creator and living in the power of the Holy Spirit.

Revelation 12:10 talks about the enemy being our accuser and "accusing us before God day and night." It says that he's been thrown down "because the salvation, power, kingdom of God and the authority of Christ have come." Because Jesus saved you, you carry these things! You carry the power and kingdom of God and authority of Jesus.

Through Jesus, we can overcome the enemy and lies. Jesus has won! You are pure because of HIM.

YOUR MISSION TODAY

Say to yourself out loud three times "Jesus says I am pure." Thank Him and let that truth bless you.

In the next chapter, we will go after forgiveness and what that looks like.

CHAPTER 7

FORGIVEN AND FREE

Jesus' blood covers us and cleanses us. You might be hearing accusation and condemnation from the enemy, but it doesn't have power over you because of Jesus and what He has done for you.

We were made for God, to give HIM ALL the glory, worship, praise and honor. To be filled with Holy Spirit and be made One with Him, where He is our God and we are His children. This is what it truly means to be fully alive.

Jesus says, "This is eternal life, that they may know You, the only true God, and Jesus Christ whom You have sent." John 17:3.

FORGIVENESS IS A GIFT

There are times when we sin and choose or allow thoughts that are not of Jesus, when we let them linger or partner with them. The beautiful thing about Jesus is we can always come to Him and repent which means turn away from sin and turn to God again.

In James 5:16 it says, "Therefore, confess your sins to one another, and pray for one another, so that you may be *HEALED*. The effective prayer of a righteous man can accomplish much." And 1 John 1:9 says, "If we confess our sins, He is faithful and righteous to forgive us our sins and to cleanse us from *ALL* unrighteousness." Because of what Jesus did on the cross, we can be forgiven from all our sin. But it does require us to confess our sin and ask for forgiveness, and He will! When we come to God, we get saved, healed and delivered. We are forgiven and free.

A friend of mine told me what his family does when they ask for forgiveness from each other. They say, "You are forgiven and free." Isn't that so beautiful to say? It's like they're saying not only are you forgiven, but you're also *free from what you asked forgiveness for.*

FORGIVE WHO?

I remember a time in my mind I had a moment with Jesus. I was given the opportunity to forgive myself. I saw myself in front of me, looking at me. I chose to forgive myself and hugged myself. It was a beautiful moment and powerful to see me forgive myself. In order for me to be whole, I needed to forgive myself. Not just others, but myself as well.

It is so important to forgive yourself. To not just ask for forgiveness from God and to forgive others in your heart. Forgiving yourself is part of forgiveness.

Forgiveness brings freedom and healing to you as well as to others. When you choose not to forgive, you are the one in prison, not the other person.

I'm talking to myself when I say this as well. Remember, Jesus forgives you for all your sins so how much more do we need to forgive. If He forgave us for everything, why would we hold back forgiveness for others? If we hold back forgiveness for others, it's like saying Jesus' forgiveness is not big enough. And don't get me wrong, it can be hard to forgive others. But when I come back to this truth that He's forgiven me for EVERYTHING, there's no question but to forgive.

Luke 23:34 gets me: "But Jesus was saying, "Father, forgive them; for they do not know what they are doing."" Jesus forgives us and knows the things we've done, even if we don't know to the full extent what we have done. He sees our hearts. He sees our motives. He knows why people did what they did. He knows why you did what you did, even if you don't. Through Jesus, He can purify us so that our motives and hearts are pure in everything we think, do and say.

Jesus forgave and this is what we are called to do. To love, to forgive and follow God. It is all through the power of Holy Spirit. God is about doing good and healing all. He wants us all to live in His full freedom. And one of the ways to live in His full freedom is to forgive. If you don't forgive, you will not be fully alive in Jesus. Jesus is the only One that can help you forgive because He forgives us. He completely understands what it's like to forgive those that have wronged us. We have all wronged Jesus and He has forgiven us. Through Him, we can forgive too.

YOUR MISSION TODAY

Ask Jesus to remind you of His forgiveness for you. His love towards you. When you remember His forgiveness, ask Jesus if there is someone you need to forgive. It could be someone else and it could be forgiving yourself. Then, through the power of the Holy Spirit, forgive that person and be free in Jesus. Jesus will give you everything you need to forgive. He is so proud of you! And so am I.

In the next chapter, we will learn that we are a triune being and the different purposes of that, talk about thoughts, the light and authority.

CHAPTER 8

TRIUNE BEING

One thing I've learned is we have a spirit, soul and a body. We are one person with three parts. We are a triune being, which means consisting of three in one, made in the image of our Triune God; Father, Jesus and Holy Spirit. We really do look like Him!

Sometimes, our soul or body will want to lead our whole triune being, just like three people in a car with one of them driving. Our soul or body will want to be driving, but they are never meant to be driving or leading. They are a blessing from the Lord, but not good masters or leaders. They are meant to be good helpers.

What I have learned is I can make a declaration saying, "My spirit, lead my soul and body in Jesus name." Or pray, "Holy Spirit, lead my spirit, soul and body." This has helped me to realign with God's thoughts on how to feel and be. Our soul and body need reminders that God is God, not them. That as much as they want to protect us and lead us, they are not God. They don't see everything. They don't always see like God does. We are not meant to follow our soul or body, but to follow Holy Spirit.

To me, my spirit feels like an older lady who is secure in God and knows she is one with Him, not doubting Him at all. She has a history with God that He is faithful and takes care of her.

My soul feels like a child, who loves the Lord and delights in Him. Sometimes though it doubts, feels alone or like He's far away. My soul needs reminding that He's in me, that I'm safe in Him and He's taking care of me. My soul needs to be led and guided.

My body feels like it follows my soul, which could be like another child following the soul child. It needs guidance and to be led. It needs reminding that it's being taken care of as well. My body has my spirit and soul inside it which is an important role. I can be a human on earth as well as being a spirit and soul at the same time.

When the Lord takes us home one day, the Bible says we will get new bodies. Our body is meant to be a helper, not the leader. This is why Holy Spirit needs to lead our spirit, soul and body.

In 1 Thessalonians 5:23 it says, "Now may the God of peace Himself sanctify you entirely; and may your spirit and soul and body be preserved complete, without blame at the coming of our Lord Jesus Christ." We have a spirit, soul and body that are made to live in the peace of God. Living in God's peace changes how we think to how God thinks.

A MOMENT WITH JESUS

I have had many encounters with Jesus. When I say encounters, I mean moments with Him where He reveals His Nature to me and I get to know Him more. In these moments He speaks to me in His

Word and through pictures He shows me in my mind about Him and myself.

A couple of years ago there was a woman who was helping me find Jesus in an encounter. I saw in my mind some children that represented different emotions, thoughts and feelings. There was the fear child, the happy child, the unsure child, the insecure child, the peaceful child, etc. When she asked me are there any more, I immediately saw thousands upon thousands of children in my head and I started to weep. All of these children were representing my thoughts, feelings and emotions. I was overwhelmed but also felt known that what I was carrying and felt heavy was real. She told me to have all these children go to the Father to play with Him and He will take care of them and I can be myself without them.

This was a huge moment for me. I found out that I didn't have to be afraid of my thoughts, emotions and feelings. They were like children that needed to be fathered and covered and I could not do it. It was too heavy and I didn't feel fully alive. Only the Father could take care of them. The Father was setting me free in a way that was beautiful and not scary. He wanted me to be free from these "children" and for me to be my totally free self in Him without having to carry these thoughts, emotions and feelings.

The beautiful thing about encounters with Jesus is you can always go back into them with Him. He can keep encountering you in those moments. Because Jesus is outside of time and space, we can encounter Him in Holy Spirit with our renewed mind.

A way Jesus has helped me with thoughts is that when a thought comes, I give it to Jesus. I ask Him if He will take it and I picture Him saying yes and taking it and then I move on. Or I just give a thought to Jesus and trust Him to take care of it. Sometimes it's not as easy as that but a lot of times it is.

I have found it is so sweet to invite Jesus, Holy Spirit and the Father into the moment in the thoughts I'm feeling and thinking. It just creates space for God to come in, to be with me in the moment, to help and remind me He is there. It also reminds me that He is everywhere at once and sees everything. Inviting

Him into everything brings light and no hiddenness, no darkness. God already knows everything we're thinking. But when we invite Him into what's going on in the moment, it makes it come to light and reminds us that He is there with us so that there's nothing hidden.

There are times when we need to get prayer from those that love Jesus and are close to us to cover us. There are times when thoughts don't shake off as easily as other thoughts. Prayer is so powerful to get covering and bring thoughts to the light so that we are free from anything the enemy wants us to feel in bondage about. The thoughts the enemy throws at us are to distract us from God. Jesus is always THE WAY out of any thought.

Jesus is bringing us out of the habit of thinking thoughts that aren't what He thinks into how He thinks! Definitely give yourself grace in this process. God is helping us renew our minds every day to think the way He thinks.

THE LIGHT IS POWERFUL!

Psalms 36:9 says, "For with You is the fountain of life; in Your light we see light." In God's light we see light. We get to see it the way He does. And in Ephesians 5:13 it says, "But all things become visible when they are exposed by the light, for everything that becomes visible is light." The light is so powerful! When you bring something to light, you are making it become light. That's amazing! It no longer has the darkness part of it because it's in the light and becomes light. It's free from the darkness.

When you turn on a light switch in a dark room, everything becomes lit with light, there's no darkness at all. 1 John 1:5 says, "And this is the message we have heard from Him and announce to you, that God is light, and in Him there is no darkness at all." God is Light! There is no darkness in Him. AT ALL. No fear, no shame, no guilt, no evil. He is Light!

The light is SO BIG compared to darkness. It's like a human compared to an ant. Even that isn't a big enough contrast because God is so much bigger. But the human represents God and the ant represents the enemy. There is no competition. The enemy, who was Lucifer, is a creation of God while God is God. It's not like how in some movies the enemy looks like he's either the same or bigger than the good guy. In reality, GOD IS GOD and is SO much bigger than the enemy.

JESUS GAVE US AUTHORITY

Through Jesus, we have authority to say no to the enemy and command his voice to be silent. Matthew 28:18 says, "And Jesus came up and spoke to them saying, "All authority has been given to Me in heaven and on earth." Yes! Jesus has all authority because He is God, He died on the cross, rose again for us and He is victorious over the enemy and all evil. Because of Who Jesus is and what He's done, when we choose to believe in Jesus, ask Him to forgive us and fill us with Holy Spirit, HIS authority is OUR authority because HE lives in us. We are One with

Him. And this is why we can command evil and the enemy to be silent and go to the feet of Jesus because it has NO power over us anymore BECAUSE of what Jesus did and Who HE is.

You are a Warrior. You fight battles that are meant for you to fight. You are not meant to fight alone, but with Holy Spirit. He is your Victory for every battle you face. And the wars you fight are for God's Kingdom and for the kingdom of darkness to bow at the feet of Jesus!

YOUR MISSION TODAY

What is one thing that is bothering you lately in your mind? Tell that emotion, feeling or thought to go to the Father and picture you not having to take care of it anymore. Ask Holy Spirit to lead your spirit, soul and body. If you ever feel like your soul or body is leading your spirit, ask Him to realign you. Remember, we are all on a journey with Jesus. He is so proud of you! YOU'VE GOT THIS! HE'S GOT YOU!

In the next chapter, we will learn more about how God sees, knows you and understands you.

CHAPTER 9

GOD KNOWS

"I SEE YOU" GIFTS

I remember a time years ago when I went to the movie theater with my family and a twelve year old boy that was a friend of ours. He was our neighbor and almost eight years younger than me but super fun to be around. We were going to a movie called Woodlawn (which is a great movie by the way). We were in line where you could buy snacks and candy and my friend asked me what candy I liked. I told him I really like the little Butterfinger squares, and as I was finishing my sentence he ran, got the Butterfinger squares, went to the counter and bought them for me. When he asked me this question, I wasn't sure if he was asking me what candy I liked because he wanted to get me something or if he just wanted to know. I was so pleasantly surprised and blessed that he wanted to bless me in that way. He wanted to make sure it was something I liked. I felt so seen and loved by him. This reminded me of how God sees and loves me personally and freely. This boy was unashamed to buy me candy and he wanted to because he wanted to.

This is a great picture of how God feels about us. He wants to freely and personally bless us and He knows how to *because* He made us.

It's also a really cool picture of how boys can influence and bless more than they realize and know. Your simple acts of kindness and love go far and reflect the heart of God.

It may seem simple, but because you are made in the image of God and love Him, it is so powerful because you're under the influence of heaven and Jesus. It reminds me of a secret agent or someone who saves someone and no one knows about it. The effects of their choices and decisions bless and affect everyone else, even if they are not seen by people in the decisions they make. The decisions you make can bless people hugely. It is a reflection of the heart of God for them. You are made to bless freely and fully with Jesus!

HAVE FUN CHOOSING! WHAT DO YOU WANT?

Your Heavenly Father loves when you choose something. Picture a good earthly father having his son pick out what ice cream flavor he wants. The father doesn't tell his son which one to get, but lets his son choose. The son then chooses exactly the one he wants.

Picture this: a son that *doesn't know* who he is and looks to his father to show him which one is the father's right flavor to choose for ice cream. He thinks to himself, "If I choose the chocolate flavor, will he be more pleased or would he be more pleased if I chose the strawberry flavor?"

A good earthly father would want his son to choose, no matter what the flavor would be, because the father wants his son to choose what he truly wants. The father wants his son to be himself.

Even though our Heavenly Father knows what we like before we know what we like, He loves the discovery of us figuring out who we are and what we like. He loves doing life with us, as if He is finding it out with us for the first time.

God loves seeing life through our eyes. He loves discovering how we view life and why we make the decisions we make. He loves getting to know us, even though He already knows us. He loves getting to know us as we get to know ourselves. He wants to discover it with us in relationship. God is all about relationship.

It reminds me of people watching a baby walk or say something. They're so in the moment watching and enjoying the baby learn and grow. There's anticipation in their eyes for what the baby is going to learn next, what he's gonna say, what he's gonna do. They just enjoy being around the baby, seeing him enjoy life and discover what life is. People have a wonder and joy when they watch babies. I think it's because it reminds us of how God must feel about us. That's how God feels about you. He's in awe and wonder of who you are. He loves discovering you with you. He loves watching you discover life. You bring Him so much joy!

BEING MISUNDERSTOOD STINKS

God gets us. But people don't always get us. Being misunderstood stinks. I've been there too. People misunderstand us because they don't know us. Once they get to know us, they'll understand us. I believe that's a big reason why God said do not judge. Because none of us know each other like He does. We don't even fully understand ourselves. Only God does. God is the only One that truly and fully understands us.

There are times when people don't see you or hear what you have to say because they're absorbed in either themselves, what others think of them or they're just truly unaware. It's hard when people don't understand you or assume your motives and intentions are bad. When you love from your heart and then others don't understand you and assume that you did it with wrong motives, it hurts. It hurts because they are not seeing your heart as pure. They're not seeing you for who you really are.

Jesus absolutely knows what it's like to be misunderstood. People misunderstood Him all the time. The thing is, only God knows what's going on in people's hearts. He's the only One that truly understands and sees the intentions and motives of the heart. He understands why we do what we do, why we say what we say and why we think what we think. That is why it's so important to invite Holy Spirit into the moment when you're hurting or don't feel understood by people because He gives you the ability to forgive. And remember, we're all on a journey. We all need God.

God sees you. He sees the things that have hurt you. He understands being hurt, and He understands you. He knows where you're coming from. He knows and understands you more than you know and understand yourself. It's beautiful to have the One that created you to be the One that fully understands and gets you. You are understood. God gets you!

LET GOD LOVE YOU

Some of my biggest breakthroughs happen when I let God love me. These often happen in times of worship at church, putting on music I find God in, or reading His word that describes God's heart and speaks to me about His love for me.

I remember a time in worship when God's love hit me and I started to weep. I felt His love for me. It was so real and deep. I let God love me. I let Him reveal His heart to me. I was getting to feel His heart for me and allow Him to pour His love in my heart.

I encourage you to let God love you. Whether that's listening to a song while closing your eyes and letting the words sing over you of His heart for you, or reading His word and letting the truth of His heart speak to you.

These deep moments of God are a part of your portion. Bringing alignment to *why* you are here and *how* much you are loved. He loves you because God is love. (1 John 4:8)

YOUR MISSION TODAY

God loves you and knows you. He lets you know He does in many ways. Ask God to give you awareness of His special and personal gifts that He gives you every day. When you are aware of a gift He gives you, take a moment to see how it made you feel and thank Him for it. Get ready to be blessed and amazed at how He knows you!

In the next chapter, we will learn about sons and fathers, what the Good Father and friendship with Him look like.

CHAPTER 10

SONS AND FATHERS

Some sons don't have good fathers. But praise the Lord that God can do anything! He can heal father wounds, heal broken relationships and bring forgiveness and comfort where there's pain.

The Lord is the Good Father and is more than able to be your Father, heal your earthly father and earthly fathers that represent a father to you. When the Father sent the Son Jesus to be the Savior of the world, He was thinking of you. Truly! He saw that you would need a good earthly father.

For those that don't have good earthly fathers, He came to show that He is the Good Father and always will be. God can stand in the gap as your Father and show you what a father is like. He came for those that have good earthly fathers too, because no father is perfect but our Heavenly Father. Our earthly father is meant to be a reflection of our Heavenly Father.

In the Bible you see time and time again God being such a Good Father to the Israelites and other nations. He guided them, forgave them, and for their good, shared with them what would happen if they followed Him and what would happen if they didn't follow Him. He shared with them what would happen depending on their choice, clear and kind, just like a good earthly father would. He was always drawing them closer to Him and at the same time, gave them a choice to choose Him or not. They were not His prisoners or captives. He wanted them to follow Him out of their own will and choice, not out of manipulation or force.

LIFE OR DEATH?

There is a really cool passage in the Bible where God is talking to the Israelites about choosing life or death and what the outcomes would be depending on their choice. He also highlights the one He wants them to choose – Life.

God says, ""See, I have set before you today life and prosperity, and death and adversity; in that I command you today to love the Lord your God, to walk in His ways and to keep His commandments...I have set before you life and death, the blessing and the curse. So choose LIFE in order that you may live, you and your descendants, by loving the Lord your God, by obeying His voice, and by holding fast to Him; for this is your life..." Deuteronomy 30:15-16,19-20.

Following God is where true life is. If you want to truly live, follow God because you were made for Him. What He says is life and is for you. God is always for you, never against you. When He says something is life, it is truly life, even if it's hard to do. He doesn't lie to us, He reveals the truth to us because He is the Truth. (John 14:6) He cannot lie (Titus 1:2). What He has for us and wants for us is to bring us close to Him and reflect His Nature, to know Him and be like Him through Holy Spirit. We can only be like God through Holy Spirit and what Jesus did on the cross for us. It is possible with God.

The amazing thing about God and His ways too is when you love God, it is fun to obey Him. It's not obeying a master, it's obeying and following the One you love the most. Knowing He is for you and loves you with everything He is makes it a joy to love God back with all that we are through Holy Spirit. There is nothing greater or better than to be One with God and get to love Him back with the love He loves us with!

WHAT DO YOU KNOW AND SHOW?

In John 5:19, Jesus says that He does what His Father is doing. This reminds me that when we see what our earthly fathers do, we learn to do the same things they are doing. Fathers have a power to disciple and teach their kids, even without the father knowing it. Sons watch their fathers and are learning what it is to be a man through what their father says, does, and what he believes and thinks about life. They're learning how a man treats his wife, how he treats his kids, and how he treats people he knows and doesn't know. He teaches both knowingly and unknowingly.

Sometimes fathers don't grow up knowing God so they just grow up knowing what their earthly father showed them and taught them. Then they teach their kids what they know and what they have been shown because they don't know any different. God can redeem anyone and anything. He sees and understands why we do what we do. There is always hope with God.

This is why it is so important to see what Jesus says about Himself and the Father. Because the Father and Jesus are God and our Creator. We were always meant to reflect Them, to do what They are doing. In John chapters 5, 6 and 8, Jesus talks about Himself and the Father in depth, Their roles and how They honor each other. If you're interested and want to go deeper, I encourage you to look at these chapters to get the heart of Jesus and the Father in

Their roles as Son and Father. We can learn from Them how to treat God, ourselves and others like They treat each other.

SHOW AND TELL

Have you ever wondered what God thinks of you? Imagine yourself as a creator of something. It could be a car, toy, food, animal, etc. Imagine your creation wanting to know what you think of it. And imagine you wanting to let your creation know what you think of it as well. Both of you are curious and wondering what the other thinks of them. The only way the other will know what you think of them is if you SHOW them and TELL them. The creator knows what they have created. The creation doesn't always know what the creator thinks of it UNLESS the creator puts identity in them or tells them who they are. To God, you are precious in His sight and He loves you! (Isaiah 43:4) He is your Creator and Father. (1 John 3:1) He thinks of you all the time. (Psalm 139:17-18) And oh how well He thinks of you!

GOD'S GREATNESS

The chapters Job 38 through 41 are incredible! I encourage you to read them. They are about God talking to Job about things He has made and God is seeing if Job remembers Who made all these things. I love these chapters because it shows the wonderful expanse and beauty of God, how He made things and what He says about them. He is reminding Job that He is God and that Job is a creation of His. We need these reminders. It reminds us of the greatness of God, our Creator and the Creator of all.

When we are afraid, it's a signal letting us know that we're forgetting how amazing God is. We're forgetting that He is good and right here with us. When we remember God, fear leaves because it is WAY smaller than God. Our problem is not how people view us or what we think about others. It's not even about our expectations being met or unmet. These things fall into the right place when we remember God and how great He is.

YOUR MISSION TODAY

What is something today you can tell God that you love about Him? You can speak it out loud or write down three things that you love about God and why. Thank Him for who He is and how He shows Himself to you. Then, ask Him what He loves about you and write it down. Say it out loud over yourself in front of a mirror.

In the next chapter, we will learn about some of the amazing gifts God has given you.

CHAPTER 11

GIFTS YOU CARRY

AWARENESS GIFT

There have been times in my life where boys have really blessed my walk with God. I have seen and felt God's Presence through their lives and I felt His heart for them and also His heart for me. I have felt the compassion of Jesus through their eyes, their hug, their awareness of something that I needed or enjoyed. It made me feel known, seen, loved and worthwhile. This reminds me how it feels when you realize God sees you and has always had an awareness of your needs and what you enjoy. He created you that way to enjoy Him forever and to find all that you need is in *Him*.

I remember a time when my neighbor friends and I were riding rip-stiks which is like skateboarding but a little different. I turned too fast and fell flat on my back and all the air got knocked out of me. I was scared and couldn't talk and so I crawled over to the grass area. Two of my friends, one of them being a boy, came over to me and were checking on me to see how I was. I felt so loved and covered by them. When they came to me, it showed me that they cared about me and were aware of what was happening. That made me feel very loved.

There is a beautiful power God has given boys to be aware of others. It is connected to the power of God because God is aware of us and cares about us. It reminds us of who God is, that He would come at the drop of a hat and see how we are doing. The beautiful thing about God is He is ALWAYS there even before something happens.

UMBRELLA COVERING GIFT

Boys also have the gift to cover. They have this feeling of covering like an umbrella over a person, this ability to protect, to shade, to comfort, and the feeling of the presence that someone is there with them. They give this ability for people to feel safe, covered, protected and not alone, without them even trying. It's a gift. The boy's presence gives empowerment to the other person. They have the ability to know and to let people know that they are worthwhile. Their presence is like a hug from Jesus. What a wonderful gift this is.

In order for boys to cover well, they need to be covered well. When a boy covers well, you know that he has experienced this by Jesus and hopefully by his parents too. When a boy doesn't cover well or isn't even aware that he carries this, it could be because he was never taught it or shown it. The Lord is so good at making us aware, bringing people into our lives that can cover us and reflect the Father to us. Then we will be able to cover others as we are made to.

STEADY GIFT

You also have this amazing gift of being steady like a foundation. You have the ability to cover like an umbrella but you also have the gift of being a stable foundation as well. The gift of covering someone from their head to their feet. Covering the whole person. God has given you this ability to make a person feel safe. This is a great gift. When things feel unsure or unsafe, you can come in and bring safety with the umbrella covering and steadiness in the midst of a storm. You can provide shelter, safety, peace, reassurance and protection.

The umbrella covering is like a hug but the steady foundation gift is like a consistent provision. Others don't realize the depth of what you bring sometimes because it's so consistent and safe. Because you bring this consistency and safety, others don't have to even think about it because you bring it.

A GIFT WE CAN GIVE YOU

Boys need space and time to think, process and choose. For them to hear God through someone or just on their own. To find out what they're made of. What they're made for. What they're interested in. What they don't like. They need to experience what it's like to make decisions.

It's really honoring to them when we give them space to process and say their thoughts. If we give them space and time, we'll get to know the real them. They also might find out more of who they are when they have time to process what they think.

When you give boys and men the ability to speak, they find out things about themselves they might not have known and you get to know them truly and better. When you give them space to process, think and speak, it gives them safety to be their full selves and find out more of who they are and what they think about. About life, everything.

When you show interest in them and what they have to say, it gives them the ability to share freely and find out what's inside of them. When you give them space to process and speak, you are actually giving them honor and the ability to be their full selves. You find out wisdom and treasure that is stored in them that God put in their heart that is food for you as well as for them.

Giving them space gives them a sense that they are worthwhile and matter to you. That what they have to say and think matters. The Bible says be quick to hear, slow to speak and slow to anger. (James 1:19) This is where all these things come into play with boys and men. To truly listen. To be slow to speak. You get the most fruit out of them when you do these things. Be quick to listen. To truly be present in the moment. To truly listen as if you were listening to Jesus. Because when we honor each other, we honor Jesus.

When we are quick to hear, listen and slow to speak, we will be slow to get angry because we are listening. When we interrupt or don't give them enough space to process, then we interrupt the flow of us getting to know the true them and them getting to know the true them as well.

We can always ask for people to give us moments to process and share so they are aware of what we need. This can be really helpful for you and others so you can be heard well and they get to know you better.

YOUR MISSION TODAY

What gift spoke the most to you? Ask God to give you a person today that you can practice this gift on.

In the next and final chapter, I want to invite you into something.

CHAPTER 12

INVITATION

In 1 John 2:13-14 it says, "I am writing to you, fathers, because you know Him who has been from the beginning. I'm writing to you, young men, because you have overcome the evil one. I have written to you, children, because you know the Father. I have written to you, fathers, because you know Him who has been from the beginning. I've written to you, young men, because you are strong, and the word of God abides in you, and you have overcome the evil one."

These verses are my heart for you too. You know Him who has been from the beginning. You have overcome the evil one. You know the Father. You are strong. The word of God abides in you. All these things are important for you to know for the rest of your life. I hope and pray that this book has deepened your walk with God and reminded you how much Jesus loves you. You are important to God. You are why He came. You have a purpose. God made you on purpose, for His glory and your good. You are made to know Him, love Him and share Him with all.

You are stronger than you know. Stronger than you realize. You are made to reflect what the Father, Jesus and Holy Spirit are like through your life, to know your identity in Jesus, the Father and Holy Spirit. You are incredibly loved by God. Forever. That will never change.

BEST DECISION EVER

I want to invite you into something. You've been reading about how God sees you and what Jesus has done for us. His desire for us to see like He sees again. I want you to know that Jesus died for you too. He died for the whole world; for those who have gone, those that are alive right now, and those that will come. He did it once for all (1 Peter 3:18). Once, for all. Jesus is the Savior of the world. He came to save you from sin and eternal death, life without Him. We all have sinned. We all need Jesus. There's not one of us that doesn't. Jesus was the only One that could save us from sin, spiritual death and broken relationship with God forever. Jesus never sinned and is God's Son and that is why He is the only One who could save us and bring us back to God. (2 Corinthians 5:21 and John 3:16). Jesus is the Way, the Truth and the Life (John 14:6) and He has come to bring you back into oneness with God, seeing as He sees, living in right relationship with Him forever. He did it.

But in order for you to live in this gift, you need to receive it. If you want a relationship with Jesus, forgiveness of all your sins and to be made a new creation as the Bible says, Jesus made a way for you. He is the Way. There is no other way but through Jesus to be made right with God. (John 3:16) I want to invite you into this free gift of God that brings you eternal life, to be forgiven, free and filled with Holy Spirit and one day, live in heaven with

Jesus forever and all those that believe in Him. (1 Thessalonians 4:13-18)

Do you want Jesus? Do you believe in Jesus? Do you want to be forgiven and free? Do you want to be filled with Holy Spirit? Do you want to be made new and clean? What the Bible says is for us to believe in the Lord Jesus and we will be saved. (Acts 16:31) A way you can do that is by praying a prayer of your own words or with me in this prayer below. Prayer is talking with and to God.

Jesus, I believe You died on the cross for me, that You were buried and rose again to forgive me of all my sin and make me one with You again. I ask You to come into my life, forgive me of all my sin, fill me with Holy Spirit and make me a new creation. Save, heal and deliver me. Thank You for loving me, choosing me and bringing me back into right relationship with You. You are my Lord, my Savior and I believe in You. I will follow You. In Jesus name, amen.

If you prayed this prayer or prayed a prayer like this to God, the Bible says we are brothers and sisters in Christ! You are part of the family of God. A child of God. (1 John 3:1) A son of God. (Galatians 3:26) You are a new creation; the old has gone and the new has come! (2 Corinthians 5:17) Through Jesus and what He did, we are made new. Jesus has given us the Holy Spirit because without Him, as we have read, we could not live this life victoriously. But with Holy Spirit, we can live like Jesus lived; victoriously and one with God forever. Thank You Jesus!

A BLESSING

I bless you in the name of Jesus. I bless you to receive everything God died for you to receive. I bless you to experience, know, believe and love Jesus with all you are. I bless you in your seeking Him that you will find Him and you will find who you are as you seek Him. You are strong, courageous, made to be alive, made to grow and learn, made to find God and find your peace in Him and live from that place. You are made to empower. You are made as a boy, young man and man to grow in the ways of God. To know Him. To love Him. To find Him in everything. To seek Him with all your heart, soul, mind and strength. You are made to have Jesus be your Ultimate Joy. To find healing, satisfaction and fulfillment in Jesus. He is the wholeness you are looking for. He is the One who knows you and made you. He is so proud of you. And so am I.

I bless you as your sister in Christ to know that you are mighty in Jesus. He is giving you everything you need to live life victoriously and joyfully. You are made to live for God and with Him forever. You are made to worship Him all of your days and into eternity with Him forever. You are His delight. You are His joy. You are why He came. You are alive right now because of the love of Jesus, Father and Holy Spirit. He has blessed you. He has washed you clean. He has made you whole. He has filled you with Holy Spirit. He is the power that you live from. You will never live a day without Him. Because He always was, He always is and He always will be.

The world needs you. It needs boys, young men and men that are following and in love with Jesus. Sold out for Him. Following Him. Showing them what it looks like to be a child of God and a son of God. Whole, forgiven and free. Kind, forgiving, loving, humble, gentle and strong. You are made to give them Jesus. To love them like He does. To follow in His footsteps. To follow His example.

You are His child, His son. You are forever chosen by Him. You are forever loved by Him. Nothing can ever separate you from His love. (Romans 8:38-39)

Now go in the peace of Jesus, the comfort of the Holy Spirit and in the power of Almighty God. He is with you, in you and around you. You've got this because He's got you. Be strong and courageous! Do not be afraid or discouraged. For the Lord your God is with you wherever you go. (Joshua 1:9)

If you have any more questions about Jesus or want to chat about any of this, feel free to reach out to *issacharjesusbooks@gmail.com*.

I bless you to know and be filled with Holy Spirit overflowing with His love and awareness. I bless you to follow Him all the days of your life. I bless you to enjoy Him forever. Keep seeking Him; He is what life is all about. :)

EXTRAS

SOME THOUGHTS TO HELP YOU GROW IN JESUS

As a new believer, remember to give yourself grace as you grow in Jesus. When the Bible talks in John 3 about being born again, it's talking about being born again in the kingdom of God and living in His ways. Just like when you were born as a baby, you learned how to eat and needed help with everything. And that's the same when you follow Jesus. When you first believe in Him, you are like a baby again in the kingdom of God spiritually. So you will be growing in your maturity, knowledge and love of God as you grow in Jesus. You will learn to eat more "solid food", learn how to honor God and others, take care of yourself and how to love and take care of others like Jesus did (Hebrews 5:12-14, Colossians 3:12-17, 1 Corinthians 13, Romans 12, Ephesians 4:11-32…). This life is a journey and adventure with Jesus. You get to know and love God more every day. And not only that, you get to know more that you are known and loved by God every day. :)

I encourage you to read the Bible because that is where you get to know Him the best. God spoke to people who followed Him and they wrote it down. The Bible is something you don't just read once, you read it for the rest of your life. What I like to do is read a chapter a day and a couple verses at night before I go to bed. Holy Spirit will lead you what to read and you get to choose too. You can read as much as you want too! The Bible is a great book to binge! It can be more than one chapter, a Bible plan, the same chapter or verse soaking in it for a while etc. I've even read the New Testament backwards as in reading from Revelation to Matthew instead of Matthew to Revelation.

Matthew, Mark, Luke and John, are called the Gospels in the Bible and are all about Jesus and His life and what He did so those are always good to read. They are about the New Covenant through Jesus. The books after these books are when Jesus went into heaven and what God did with people after that.

Matthew to the last book Revelation is the New Testament. And the books before the four gospel books are the Old Testament, before Jesus came and set us free from the law of sin and fulfilled the law of the Old Covenant. It's also about the works of God and how He loved people in the midst of their choices and gave them outcomes of what it would look like if they chose Him and if they chose their own way.

Proverbs is in the middle of the Bible and it's full of wisdom and instruction. It's a father giving his son instruction. It also talks about the difference between one that follows God - the righteous - and the wicked - one who doesn't follow God. There are 31 chapters so you could read one a day in a month.

All of the Bible speaks God's heart and love for us with Holy Spirit. He will speak to you. The Bible reminds me of a treasure hunt, where with Holy Spirit you are finding out in His Word how much He loves you. About His Faithfulness to never stop loving you, and to keep chasing after you.

The Bible is all about God being the Hero and making Himself low to save us and bring us back to Him, His children that are no longer lost but found. It's all about our Heavenly Father bringing back His kids to Himself, Who they are made for. It's about God's desire for us to know and love Him through Him knowing and loving us. He knows and loves us. He spoke to people back then, but the beautiful thing about God's Word is that it's alive so it speaks to us today too.

Hebrews 4:12 - "For the word of God is living and active and sharper than any two-edged sword, and piercing as far as the division of soul and spirit, of both joints and marrow, and able to judge the thoughts and intentions of the heart."

There are so many layers to God's Word, depths of revelation and life. He speaks to us in every season of life. And in different seasons, different parts of His Word speak to us and are what we need in that season. If you have any questions about the Bible, God, Jesus, or want prayer, feel free to contact me. I'd be happy to help.

GOD SPEAKING TO BOYS

Years ago, God showed me His tender heart toward boys and what they carry. This part was written by the much younger me. I want you to hear what He told me. You bless His heart! Feel free to mark places that speak to you.

Boys in My Eyes from God:

"Boys are strong, competent. Lovely and beautiful in every way. They have a power that I have given to only them - love with humility, purity with strength, and hope, so much hope. They have more power than they know, more power to love, to forgive, to pioneer, to set free, to be leaders of their own life with Me and leaders of community, a society, a generation, their families.

When they draw close to Me, that's when they get stronger, because I am their Strength. Their strength comes from Me and Me alone. They don't have the power to do what they are called to do and be who they are made to be without Me. Only with Me can they do anything. Only with Me can they be who they fully are and who they were made to be and who they were made to become.

I am the Source of Life. I am the Source of their identity and without Me, they can't do anything. But with Me, they can do anything because I am their Source, because I am their Strength. I will sustain them. I will give them hope. I will give them vision and clarity, peace of mind, hope for the future, joy in the present, revelation, a fixed gaze upon Me in what I am about and what I love. I will give them one heart and way, that they may fear Me always, for their own good and for the good of their children after them. (Jeremiah 32:39)

My love for them never runs out and never runs dry. It always pursues, succeeds, and does its mission, pursues its mission till it is accomplished. There is no mission impossible because I am the God of Possibility and I am the God of Possible, making impossible possible. The love I have for them is the love they will love Me with and love others with. That is their secret. That is what their secret is - My love for them is their strength, and from that place of Me pouring out My love, they love Me in return and love others as well.

I have given them power over their words. Their words mean more than anything else that could say something. Their words, besides Mine, are more powerful than they know. The words they use, how they use it, their body language, their eye contact. What they say matters, so they could say a few words or they could say a lot, and it's powerful, because they are made in My image, made in the image of God, made in the image of their Father, where their words reflect My words, and so the words they use have power because they are reflecting Me.

The things they choose to do impact nations. They impact the world, they impact worlds. What they choose impacts everything and affects everything. Boys leave a mark. They leave a mark in this world meant for the better, but it can be for the worse. But, they are meant for the better.

What boys do matters, and it blesses My heart and reflects My heart. My heart for them and their heart for Me. They don't fully realize the power that I've given them, and the love I have for them and the love they have for Me until they move in action. When they do something with what I've given them, then they will see My love for them, their love for Me and their identity in Me - the identity I placed in them, and also the identity I have given to others in power.

They have power to empower. Boys have power to empower that is a huge gift that I've given to them that is unique, special and gives Me glory. Once they know that they are empowered by Me, they will truly empower with all their heart. Before they know they have the power to empower, they empower without knowing it because that is in their DNA, their nature, their identity that I have made them in My image.

Once they fully know their identity in Me, that they were made to empower and have the power to empower through Me, they will do it with all their heart, and it will affect even more because they have the knowledge that they are doing it with Me, and that they have identity solidified that they are made to empower through My power. They truly leave a mark meant for the better. They are meant to leave a mark for the better. They are meant to empower with My power. They are meant to give words of life that break things down that need to be broken down, that build things up that need to be built up, that draw people closer, that help people be solidified in their identities in Me.

Their words are like honey, honey is sticky, and once you get covered in honey, it's hard to get it off for a little while. Psalm 119:103 says, "How sweet are Your words to my taste! Yes, sweeter than honey to my mouth!" (This is talking about God's words but it also can apply to boys and men because you are made in God's image.) It smells good, it tastes good, but it is sticky, and that is the way their words are. The way I made their words is honey. It is sweet. It tastes good. It smells good. It's nice to be around it, but their words are sticky, and so their words will stick to you if you let it. Their words stick to you because they have power to empower. Once their words are released, it can stick to you and affect you, whether good or bad, and when it's good, it's awesome. It's made to glorify Me.

I speak with words and things are accomplished and same with boys - they speak with words and things are accomplished. They can build up and they can tear down with their words. With their words, they can empower people and with their words they can take things down that are meant to come down. They give life to things that need life, and they speak life to things that are dead that need to come to life. They also have the power like Me to speak words and for things to die that need to die.

I have given them the ability to have joy in the midst of trials that overcomes and astonishes anything that comes their way, just like Jesus, how He had joy in the midst of the journey to the cross. It astounded people the way He lived, and the way

He lived was One with His Father. That is the gift I give to boys. It is for oneness with Me, joy in the child's knowing that I am their Father and I am with them in it. That I am going to bring good out of trials, and that's why they can have joy because I am in it. I am with them and I will make it all for good.

They have the ability to sustain others like I sustain them. They reflect My image of sustaining. Their smile is the smile of God, and they can allow people to sense and feel God's smile through their smile when boys truly live in their full identity in Me. Oh, what a wonderful, joyful, beautiful sight it is to see My boys living in total freedom, identity, and love of Me, in Me. Ah, it is what they were made for, identity in Me, Oneness in Me, Oneness with Me, One Presence, them and I together forever."

ACKNOWLEDGMENTS

I want to thank my heavenly Father, Jesus and Holy Spirit for putting this book and subject on my heart and helping me accomplish and finish it well. All for Your glory God.

I want to thank my wonderful parents, Carrie and Pete Nichols and my sister Manasseh for reading my book and editing it. For cheerleading me and helping me make this book excellent. Thank you for loving me like Jesus does and showing me what He is like.

I want to thank all my family and friends that prayed for me and blessed this book.

I want to thank Havilah's Author School for teaching me steps on how to finish my first rough draft of my book and thoughts on publishing.

I want to thank my friend Jennifer Miskov for her Writing in the Glory workshop, steps for self publishing and prayers.

I want to thank my friend Maddie Cabibbo for her amazing art for my book cover. She captured my heart for the book – the bigness and closeness of God with boys and men.

ENDNOTES

CHAPTER 1 - WHAT AM I HERE FOR? WHAT IS MY PURPOSE?

ASK AND RECEIVE
GOD IS WHO AND WHAT YOU ARE LOOKING FOR. HIS REST IS GROWTH.
Ephesians 2:10 NASB 1960, 1962, 1963, 1968, 1971, 1972, 1973, 1975, 1977, 1995
Romans 8:28 NASB (paraphrased but like NASB 1995) 1960, 1962, 1963, 1968, 1971, 1972, 1973, 1975, 1977, 1995
Luke 2:26a NASB 1960, 1962, 1963, 1968, 1971, 1972, 1973, 1975, 1977, 1995
John 14:16-17 NASB 1960, 1962, 1963, 1968, 1971, 1972, 1973, 1975, 1977, 1995

CHAPTER 2 - GOD WILL INSTRUCT YOU IN THE WAY TO GO

JESUS' WAY = HONOR
YOU ARE A FULL PERSON
AM I ON THE RIGHT PATH?
JESUS SET ME FREE
Psalm 32:8 NIV 1973, 1978, 1984, 2011
Hebrews 4:12 NIV 1973, 1978, 1984, 2011
John 1:1 paraphrased
Luke 2:51-52 NASB 1960, 1962, 1963, 1968, 1971, 1972, 1973, 1975, 1977, 1995
Matthew 11:30 NASB 1960, 1962, 1963, 1968, 1971, 1972, 1973, 1975, 1977, 1995
Bill Johnson concept in my own words about the acorn and oak tree
Oswald Chambers devotional reference - *My Utmost for His Highest* (March 20, Friendship with God)

CHAPTER 3 - YOUR WORDS MATTER AND HAVE POWER

YOU ARE VERY GOOD
BELIEVE OR NOT?
WHAT WILL YOU DO?

Proverbs 18:21 KJV 1769

Proverbs 18:21 MSG 1993, 2002, 2018

Genesis 1 and 2 paraphrased

Genesis 2:7-8 paraphrased

Genesis 1:26-31 paraphrased

Psalm 139:14-16 NASB 1960, 1962, 1963, 1968, 1971, 1972, 1973, 1975, 1977, 1995

Luke 1:20 paraphrased

Luke 1:63-79 paraphrased

Luke 1:38 NASB 1960, 1962, 1963, 1968, 1971, 1972, 1973, 1975, 1977, 1995

1 Corinthians 10:31 NASB 1960, 1962, 1963, 1968, 1971, 1972, 1973, 1975, 1977, 1995

Matthew 25:37-40 NASB 1960, 1962, 1963, 1968, 1971, 1972, 1973, 1975, 1977, 1995

Luke 1:37 NASB 1960, 1962, 1963, 1968, 1971, 1972, 1973, 1975, 1977, 1995

Matthew 19:26 NASB 1960, 1962, 1963, 1968, 1971, 1972, 1973, 1975, 1977, 1995

"God doesn't make duplicates." - Francis Anfuso quote

CHAPTER 4 - BOY AND MAN

CAN IT GET ANY BETTER?! NOPE!

JESUS AS A HUMAN

DRAWN TO HIS NAME

Philippians 2:1-13 NASB 1960, 1962, 1963, 1968, 1971, 1972, 1973, 1975, 1977, 1995

Colossians 1:15-20 NASB 1960, 1962, 1963, 1968, 1971, 1972, 1973, 1975, 1977, 1995

John 14:6 paraphrased

Colossians 2:9-10 NASB 1960, 1962, 1963, 1968, 1971, 1972, 1973, 1975, 1977, 1995

John 1:16 NASB 1960, 1962, 1963, 1968, 1971, 1972, 1973, 1975, 1977, 1995

Ephesians 4:13 NASB 1960, 1962, 1963, 1968, 1971, 1972, 1973, 1975, 1977, 1995

Revelation 4:8 (part of the verse) NASB 1960, 1962, 1963, 1968, 1971, 1972, 1973, 1975, 1977, 1995

Isaiah 6:3 NASB 1960, 1962, 1963, 1968, 1971, 1972, 1973, 1975, 1977, 1995

Luke 2:40 NASB 1960, 1962, 1963, 1968, 1971, 1972, 1973, 1975, 1977, 1995

1 Timothy 4:12 NASB 1960, 1962, 1963, 1968, 1971, 1972, 1973, 1975, 1977, 1995

CHAPTER 5 - IDENTITY AND POWER AS A MAN

JESUS KNOWS THINGS
PROTECTOR AND PROVIDER
GENTLENESS IS A POWER
Luke 3:21-23 NASB 1960, 1962, 1963, 1968, 1971, 1972, 1973, 1975, 1977, 1995
John 2:23-25 NASB 1960, 1962, 1963, 1968, 1971, 1972, 1973, 1975, 1977, 1985
Matthew 26:41 NASB 1960, 1962, 1963, 1968, 1971, 1972, 1973, 1975, 1977, 1995
Genesis 1 and 2 paraphrased
Psalm 18:35c NASB 1960, 1962, 1963, 1968, 1971, 1972, 1973, 1975, 1977, 1995
Galatians 5:22-23 paraphrased
Romans 2:4 NASB 1960, 1962, 1963, 1968, 1971, 1972, 1973, 1975, 1977, 1985
Matthew 11:28-30 NASB 1960, 1962, 1963, 1968, 1971, 1972, 1973, 1975, 1977, 1985

CHAPTER 6 - JESUS HAS MADE YOU SO PURE!

STUPID LIES!
YOU MAKE THE ENEMY SCARED!
Matthew 5:8 NASB 1960, 1962, 1963, 1968, 1971, 1972, 1973, 1975, 1977, 1985
John 10:10 NASB 1960, 1962, 1963, 1968, 1971, 1972, 1973, 1975, 1977, 1985
Revelation 12:10 NASB 1960, 1962, 1963, 1968, 1971, 1972, 1973, 1975, 1977, 1985

CHAPTER 7 - FORGIVEN AND FREE

FORGIVENESS IS A GIFT
FORGIVE WHO?
John 17:3 NASB 1960, 1962, 1963, 1968, 1971, 1972, 1973, 1975, 1977, 1995
James 5:16 NASB 1960, 1962, 1963, 1968, 1971, 1972, 1973, 1975, 1977, 1985
1 John 1:9 NASB 1960, 1962, 1963, 1968, 1971, 1972, 1973, 1975, 1977, 1985
Luke 23:34 NASB 1960, 1962, 1963, 1968, 1971, 1972, 1973, 1975, 1977, 1995
You are forgiven and free quote from my friend

CHAPTER 8 - TRIUNE BEING

A MOMENT WITH JESUS

THE LIGHT IS POWERFUL!

JESUS GAVE US AUTHORITY

1 Thessalonians 5:23 NASB 1960, 1962, 1963, 1968, 1971, 1972, 1973, 1975, 1977, 1995

Psalm 36:9 NASB 1960, 1962, 1963, 1968, 1971, 1972, 1973, 1975, 1977, 1995

Ephesians 5:13 NASB 1960, 1962, 1963, 1968, 1971, 1972, 1973, 1975, 1977, 1995

1 John 1:5 NASB 1960, 1962, 1963, 1968, 1971, 1972, 1973, 1975, 1977, 1995

Matthew 28:18 NASB 1960, 1962, 1963, 1968, 1971, 1972, 1973, 1975, 1977, 1995

Denise Wakefield quote. A prayer - "Holy Spirit, lead my spirit, soul and body in Jesus name."

"When you bring something to light, you are making it become light." - Carrie Nichols quote

CHAPTER 9 - GOD KNOWS

"I SEE YOU" GIFTS

HAVE FUN CHOOSING! WHAT DO YOU WANT?

BEING MISUNDERSTOOD STINKS

LET GOD LOVE YOU

1 John 4:8 paraphrased

"I SEE YOU" GIFTS part - story of my friend Samuel Farmer

Ice cream story - Pete Nichols story

CHAPTER 10 - SONS AND FATHERS

LIFE OR DEATH?

WHAT DO YOU KNOW AND SHOW?

SHOW AND TELL

GOD'S GREATNESS

Deuteronomy 30:15-16,19-20 NASB 1960, 1962, 1963, 1968, 1971, 1972, 1973, 1975, 1977, 1995

John 14:6 paraphrased

Titus 1:2 paraphrased

John 5:19 paraphrased

John 5, 6 and 8 paraphrased
Isaiah 43:4 paraphrased
1 John 3:1 paraphrased
Psalm 139:17-18 paraphrased
Job 38 - 41 paraphrased

CHAPTER 11 - GIFTS YOU CARRY

AWARENESS GIFT
UMBRELLA COVERING GIFT
STEADY GIFT
A GIFT WE CAN GIVE YOU
James 1:19 NASB 1960, 1962, 1963, 1968, 1971, 1972, 1973, 1975, 1977, 1995
Story of neighborhood friends Samuel Farmer and Mikaela Dunbar ripstiking with me.

CHAPTER 12 - INVITATION

BEST DECISION EVER
A BLESSING
1 John 2:13-14 NASB 1960, 1962, 1963, 1968, 1971, 1972, 1973, 1975, 1977, 1995
1 Peter 3:18 paraphrased
2 Corinthians 5:21 paraphrased
John 3:16 paraphrased
John 14:6 paraphrased
1 Thessalonians 4:13-18 paraphrased
Acts 16:31 NASB 1960, 1962, 1963, 1968, 1971, 1972, 1973, 1975, 1977, 1995
2 Corinthians 5:17 paraphrased
1 John 3:1 NASB 1960, 1962, 1963, 1968, 1971, 1972, 1973, 1975, 1977, 1995, 2020
Galatians 3:26 NASB 1960, 1962, 1963, 1968, 1971, 1972, 1973, 1975, 1977, 1995
Romans 8:38-39 paraphrased
Joshua 1:9 NLT 1996, 2004, 2007, 2013

EXTRAS

SOME THOUGHTS TO HELP YOU GROW IN JESUS

John 3 paraphrased

Hebrews 5:12-14 paraphrased

Colossians 3:12-17 paraphrased

1 Corinthians 13 paraphrased

Romans 12 paraphrased

Ephesians 4:11-32 paraphrased

Matthew paraphrased

Mark paraphrased

Luke paraphrased

John paraphrased

Proverbs paraphrased

Hebrews 4:12 NASB 1960, 1962, 1963, 1968, 1971, 1972, 1973, 1975, 1977, 1995

GOD SPEAKING TO BOYS

Jeremiah 32:39 NASB 1960, 1962, 1963, 1968, 1971, 1972, 1973, 1975, 1977, 1995

Psalm 119:103 NASB 1960, 1962, 1963, 1968, 1971, 1972, 1973, 1975, 1977, 1995

ABOUT THE AUTHOR

Issachar Nichols was born and raised in Maui, Hawaii. She grew up knowing Jesus and He became her personal Savior at five years old. Over the years, God gave her a big heart for children. She has served in children's ministries in many ways including camps, clubs and childcare. Issachar currently works at a school in Redding, California with children ages kindergarten to eighth grade. A movie aficionado, she also works on the side as a character actress for children's parties. She loves doing life with her family, loving the kids at the school and zooming around town in her Mini Cooper.

Feel free to reach out to Issachar at:
issacharjesusbooks@gmail.com

Issachar with Jesus Revelations podcast is on most platforms! She records revelations Jesus gives her and posts them!

To listen, scan the QR code below:

You can follow Issachar on YouTube, Facebook, Instagram and TikTok at '*Issachar Jesus Books*'.

Follow Issachar's Amazon book page at:

www.ingramcontent.com/pod-product-compliance
Lightning Source LLC
Chambersburg PA
CBHW071228090426
42736CB00014B/3009